AF486193

GUIDANCE FOR RESEARCH

PROF N.P MBANDAZAYO

Tie Publishers

USER-FRIENDLY HAND-BOOK

RESEARCH GUIDELINES FOR POST-GRADUATE STUDIES.

First edition

ISBN: 9798223824145

This book was professionally typeset by

Tie Publisher

Table of Contents

FOREWORD

USER-FRIENDLY HAND-BOOK: RESEARCH GUIDELINES FOR POST-GRADUATE STUDIES.

ABSTRACT.

The handbook contextualizes introduction and orientation of the research study and the rational for providing guidelines for honours masters and doctoral research students.

The hand book also highlights the significance of the study, research questions, hypothesis and ethical considerations of the study. Demarcation area of the study has also been included in order to address the area where data has been gathered.

Limitations of the study are always anticipated in any study. Barriers that interfere with the research process are likely to be imminent in any study. Operational definitions of terms and literature review must be highlighted in view of the fact that the researcher has to know other authors' findings and recommendations.

Research methodology in relation to research design, sampling, data gathering has been addressed along with analysing the data quantitatively and qualitatively in search of findings and recommendations of the study.

Validity and reliability has been presented to alert the researcher about the status of a reliable and validity of the questionnaire which is a probing tool in the research process.

Time frame and research funding have been included in the study. Time frame is presented to enable the researcher to plan accordingly and to know the parameters in the sampling process, in collecting the data and in analysing available data. Research funding is equally important and has been included on the bases that once the proposal is approved researcher must apply for funding. In most cases funding is available in Universities or institution where the student is registered. At times a student can apply for outside source research funding.

CHAPTER ONE.

1.1 INTRODUCTION.

The handbook that is presented in this text serves as guidelines for post-graduate studies. It has been designed in such a way as to meet the students 'needs and guide them on how to write a dissertation/thesis.

Presentation of such a book will assist honours, master's and doctoral students in the preparation and final presentation of the chosen research study. The book will not only help students but will also assist promoters in guiding the students on the preparation and the final presentation of the study.

The handbook contextualizes the various stages to be undertaken in the preparation of the study in terms of documenting the proposal, presenting the various chapters and in the preparation of the cover page of a dissertation/ thesis.

However, it is essential for the students to browse through the literature in order to be acquainted with the chosen research topic. Literature review must also reflect studies that have been undertaken locally, nationally and internationally. The student will then be able to understand what other authors research work entails in terms of their findings and recommendations likely to assist the students in their research study processes.

1.2 WHAT IS RESEARCH?

It is essential for students doing research be informed of what research entails.

P.D.Leedy & J.Ellis provide the following eight points on what research means:

Research originates with a question or a problem. By asking a question, an inquisitive researcher ignites a chain reaction that leads to the research process. Questions posed are:

- What is such a situation like?

- Why does such phenomena occur?

- What does it all mean?

Research requires a clear articulation of a goal which is interpreted as follows:

- What problem do you intend to solve?

- When do you describe your objectives in clear, concrete terms as you have a good idea of what you need to accomplish, and you are able to direct your efforts accordingly?

- Research requires a specific plan of procedure

Researchers plan their overall research design and research method in a purposeful way so that they can acquire data relevant to their research problem.

Research usually devises the principal probe into more manageable sub problem.

From a design standpoint, it is often helpful to break the main research problem into several sub problems in order to resolve the main problem.

Research is guided by the specific research problem or hypothesis.

Having stated the problem and its attendant sub problem, a researcher usually forms one or more hypotheses. A hypothesis is a reasonable guess and logical supposition. It provides a tentative explanation for phenomena under investigation.

Research accepts certain critical assumptions.

In research the assumption must be valid or else the research is meaningless. Assumptions made must be precise and must meet required outcomes of the research.

In research the assumption must be valid or else the research is meaningless, assumptions made must be precise and meet required outcomes.

Research requires the collection and interpretation of data in an attempt to solve the problem that initiated the problem.

A researcher has to divide the sub problem with reasonable questions or hypothesis and identifies the assumptions that are basic to the entire effort. The next step is to collect whatever data which seems appropriate and to organise the data in a meaningful way so that data can be interpreted relevantly to research outcomes.

Research is by its nature, cyclical.

The research process is seen by P.D. Leedy & J. Ellis as Cyclical:

FIGURE 1

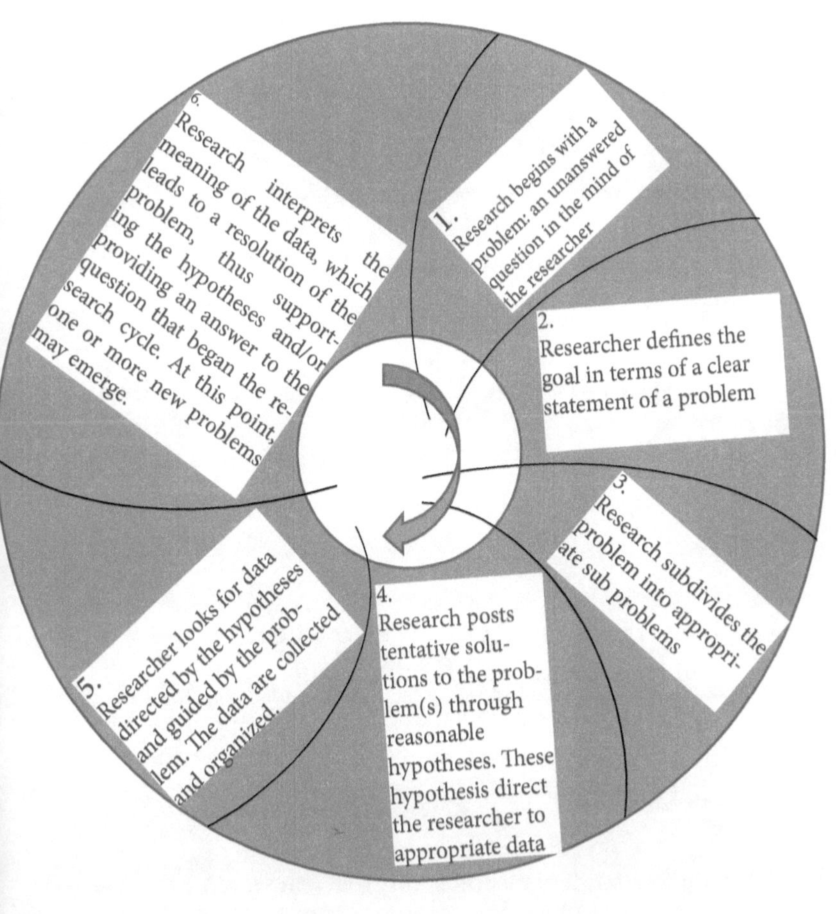

The contents of the eight phases posed by P.D. Leedy & J.Ellis (2010)can be interpreted as a guide to students in understanding the various stages that the student has to undergo. The various phases pre-determine the cycle that the student is expected to understand. As the student ventures on the start of the research program he/she is clear about the processes to undertake. The cyclical process presented above gives the student an idea of how the research evolves and develops from beginning to the end of the research.

Having discussed the cycle process of research above, below will be the discussion on the research topic. The research topic highlights the objectives of the research topic in details including sample topics that are presented to give the student an idea of what a research topic may look like in research.

1.3. OBJECTIVES OF THE RESEARCHABLE TOPICS.

- To assist post-graduate students/researchers in the selection of an appropriate topic for the research study.

- To help students prepare themselves in the writing of a research proposal.

- To make students understand that a research proposal is a preparatory and guiding stage in the writing of a dissertation/theses.

- To help students demonstrate their ability to conduct research independently.

- To help students in identifying a researchable problem.

- To make students understand that a research content in any study adds knowledge to theory.

- To provide knowledge and the skill of sampling and data gathering to students and researchers.

- To help students/researchers in quantifying data statistically, analyse, interpret and present empirical data.

- To make students understand the difference between presenting qualitative and quantitative data

- To assist students in drawing conclusions from the findings of the study.

- To guide them on how to organize a completed dissertation/theses in relation to the outlay of the study content.

- To enable students to apply technical criteria required by Universities and procedures that are followed at the completion of the study.

The following are questions to ask when selecting a research topic:

- What do you want to research?

- Why is it worthwhile to select this particular topic?

- Does the proposed topic has practical significance?

- Does the topic contribute to the community/public it serves?

- Will the topic add more value to the construction of theories about social problems?

- What are the findings and solutions of other authors on this selected topic?

In the opinion of Gray, (2009:4) there is essentially two ways of Identifying a research topic. One is through the literature, books, academic and professional journals which may raise interesting themes and topics that can be related to your interest. The second and other route is directly from the work-place or community setting.

According to Gray, et.al. (2009) avoid selecting topics that demonstrate the following areas:

- Topic that is too long which may be too clumsy to focus on the area to be researched.

- A topic which is lacking in resource material.

- Selecting a topic that is likely to damage respondents physically emotionally or intellectually.

- Selecting a meaningful topic that is not significant and is likely not to get attraction not only to the community but also to the sponsors.

• Topics that will be sensitive to race, gender and disclosure of personal information.

On the other end Jankowicz (2004) indicates that selecting a topic depends upon personal development which might include the following areas.

• Gaining access to respondents

• Speaking to the audience

• Persuading people to co-operate and

• Dealing with uncertainty about data.

Jankowicz (2004) et.al. elaborates on the above areas of selecting a topic, the subject that brings interest to the researcher involves many hours of planning, execution, data analysis and report writing. It is also of importance to choose a topic that allows the researcher to demonstrate his/her skills and abilities.

Leedy(1997), a student is supposed to discuss the importance of the researchable problem, and further be advised that they must distinguish between two basic types of problems, namely, personal problem and researchable problem. Leedy (1993) further indicates that problems may be real but not research-able. Researchable problems have to fit the requirements of the scientific method. Scientific method is the body of knowledge which is testable and proven.

Welman & Kruger (2002) are of the opinion that scientific research process is to clearly formulate the specific problem to be examined and test hypotheses stemming from such theory.

A topic can be in the form of a statement as follows e.g:

'Sources of stress on female managers and ways of coping with particular reference to Frere Hospital in East London.

Or

'A study of attitudes towards antiretroviral treatment in the Viegisville Community in Mthatha.'

A topic can also be in a question format, e.g.

'Why is poverty more prevalent in some communities than in others?

Or

What are the major factors that contribute towards crime?

A topic can also highlight a relationship between two variables e.g.

'A study on the relationship between the high Rate of Teenage Pregnancy and the child support grant.

Or

'A study on the relationship between Poverty and Crime.

A topic can also be a comparative study e.g.

'A comparative study of socio-economic life style of rural black families and urban black families.

Or

'A comparative study of the value system of the South African Black families and American black families.

Research topic of your study needs to meet the requirements of the current trend of areas to be researched. Research topics are to be relevant, focussed and significant for the study. For example, the problem of rape, violent to women and children, crime, poverty and others are significant topics which are rampant and require research.

Research topics are chosen by the researcher for a variety of the Following reasons:

* A researcher might have observed problems occurring in the community such as poverty. The problem of poverty may elicit motivation to search on poverty so that at the end of the study findings might assist the researcher to develop strategies to overcome poverty in that chosen community where research was undertaken.

- Another reason might be associated with a researcher wanting to evaluate all existing organisation, an agency or an institution. Findings of the research might provide feedback on the strengths and the weakness of the organisation.

- Third reason might be associated with searching for answer or searching for cure or remedy to HIV–AIDS epidemics.

- The researcher might require to initiate an organisation for a specific community. In that case, a researcher need to research from community members if they support the initiative. Is there a need to have for example, an institution for the orphans or the aged?

1.4. STATEMENT OF THE PROBLEM.

Problem formulation starts with a researchable topic which will develop into a systematic review of research. Ritchie & Lewis,(2003:48)& Gilbert (2008:58) support the latter view by indicating that the formulation of a research question should lead to the research methods, including the purposes and design of the study and then followed by the total research project. Babbie & Mouton (2010), Rubin & Babbie (2010), Monette, Sullivan & Dejong (2011), Royse(2011) & Thyer (2010) cite six(6) steps, namely, problem statement and research questions, research method, data collection, data analysis, interpretation of data and report writing. Rubin & Babbie further indicate that the purpose of research can be seen as part of step two(2) in research method, in which the kind of research ,the approach to research, the design, participants/subjects measuring instrument, the procedure, ethical aspects and manner of data analyses can be distinguished and logical sequence can be followed.

The purpose of research as indicated above can pose various viewpoints to knowledge. For example, Alasuutari, Brickman & Brannen, (2009:44) focus is on research strategy. Graveter & Fozano, (2012:159-167) viewpoint is on research designs. Morris,(2006:20-37) highlights objectives and other authors have other views of the purpose of research. The above terms namely research designs, strategies, purposes, objectives, and goals or aims are terms that are used interchangeable by various authors.

In problem formulation the problem presented must include a focussed practical significance of the research study in relation to the literature. Literature review to be presented briefly must include both local and abroad literature search done by various authors including authors' findings and recommendations. The literature presented in problem formulation will reflect relevantly to the research study that has to be undertaken. It also help the reader to be ready to look forward to the research study to be undertaken by the researcher.

Key areas of the current study need to be presented in clear terms. The researcher needs to elaborate on the study as a problem or as a need to undergo a study. The latter will be determined by the nature of the topic e.g. crime as a problem to society or providing health services to the aged.

Problem formulation has to reflect relevancy of the research study to be undertaken in the brief literature review. Your problem area has to indicate exactly what you need to be studying including time boundaries (when) and space boundaries (where). It is essential to make certain that what you have stated in the problem formulation is what you will be able to research. Everything you have stated in the problem formulation must be related to the interpretation of data presented.

1.5. RATIONAL FOR THE STUDY.

The study was pursued by the researcher on the basis that there was an observed problem, or a need to provide service, or to search on a specific requirement to solve the problem. The researcher wanted to seek for a solution and resulted to conducting a study in that specific area.

1.6. AIM AND THE OBJECTIVES OF THE STUDY.

1. 6.1. Aim

Aim is directed towards the research topic you have chosen as a researcher aiming at conducting the research study.

1. 6.2. Objectives

Objectives are presented in the study to determine what the researcher wants to achieve at the end of the study. Usually there are several objectives that the researcher can present. However, it is essential to limit your objectives to avoid a long winded questionnaire and also uncontrollable data that will require data analysis. Questionnaires are designed to ask questions from respondents leading to fulfilment of the objectives that you have presented in your study. It is therefore essential to present objectives that do not exceed four (4) objectives. Also the researcher must bear in mind that the last objective has to present an interventive strategy that the research would like to achieve at the end of the research study.

1.7. SIGNIFICANCE OF THE STUDY.

Significance of the study reveals the importance of the study in relation to probing and solving a persistent problem that needs attention within a given community, school, or an Institution.

1.8. RESEARCH QUESTIONS.

Research questions are directed towards the research topic to be researched. For example, you might be doing research on 'An Investigation of the causes of gender-based violence in Mqanduli Administrative Area. The following questions may be relevant:

- What does gender-violence refer to?

- Are there incidents of gender-based violence in the area? If so how prevalent?

- What is the nature of gender-based violence?

Are there any strategies and mechanisms that can possibly help to combat domestic violence in the area.

1. 9. HYPOTHESIS

Hypothesis is defined by Neuman (2006:58) as a tentative concrete testable statement about a relationship between variables. Mac Kendrick (1991:251) states that research and practice rest on a prediction of what is expected to be found. Mac Kendrick (1991:255) further indicates that hypothesis is tested by investigation and it sets a clear direction throughout the study by selecting the theory which is presented and guiding the empirical research.

According to Bless (2005:33) hypothesis is a tentative, concrete and testable statement which has the following characteristics:-

* A hypothesis should be conceptually clear

* It should be specific

* It should be empirically testable with available techniques.

A good hypothesis has variables which can be empirically explained.

According to Rubin and Babbie (1993:45) a variable is a concept's empirical counterpart. Where the concepts are in the domain of theory, variables are a matter of observation and measurement. Variables are the independent variable and the dependent variable. An independent variable is a variable that brings about a change in the other variable, the dependant variable. To cite an example Fire can be explained as an Independant variable and smoke can be presented as a dependent variable because smoke comes from out of an existing fire. Fire results to a smoke.

1.10. DEMARCATION AREA OF THE STUDY.

16

The researcher has to indicate where the study has to be conducted in the demarcation area of study is essential to provide a clear picture of the place where study has to be conducted, and relevance of the study is likely to have an impact. For example, if the study is on poverty, it might be relevant to select an area/community where poverty is rife. A student can also present a diagram which reflects the area where research will be conducted.

1.11. ETHICAL CONSIDERATIONS.

Ethics are essential in any research study when dealing with respondents.

According to Webster's new World Dictionary cited by Rubin & Babbie (2008:69) ethics is defined as conforming to the standards of conduct of a given profession or group. Whilst De Vos etal (2002) defines ethics as a set of moral principles that the group or individuals agree upon and subsequently is widely accepted, and offers rules and behavioural expectation about the most the most correct conduct towards experimental subjects and respondents, employees, sponsors and other researchers, assistant researchers and students. The researcher is therefore expected to explain in detail the issue and importance of Ethics when undertaking any research study. The following are ethical considerations to be recognised in a research study.

1.11.1. Voluntary participation

The respondents must be informed about the objectives of the study before they can participate in the research study. The researcher must get permission from respondents before collecting data from them.

1.11.2. Informed Consent

The researcher must also get a written permission from an agency, organisation, an institution a community or any demarcation area of study before undertaking research.

1.11.3. Anonymity/Confidentiality

The researcher having obtained voluntary participation from the respondents has to inform them that they will remain anonymous as their names will not appear in the questionnaire and their responses will not revealing their names. They will be assured of confidentiality and anonymity during and after the research study.

1.11.4. Deception and misrepresentation to respondents.

The researcher is expected to be honest and not to be deceptive by giving the respondents promises. It is unethical to lie to respondents.

e.g. I am conducting this research so that you will be given houses/benefits. Deceiving participants might break trust between the researcher and the respondents, and can jeopardise future research studies if promises are not fulfilled.

1.11.5. Competence of Researchers

According to De Vos et. al (2005:63) researchers are ethically obliged to ensure that they are competent and adequately skilled to undertake the proposed investigation. It is even more important that researchers must be competent especially in sensitive investigations. Even a well planned research is not competent enough when invalid results are produced.

1.11.6. Release of Publication findings

According to De Vos et. al (2005:65) findings of the study must be made known to participants. Participants must be given the respect and recognition as participants in the study and thanked by the researcher.

1.11.7. Harm to respondents.

According to De Vos et. al (2005:57) it is the responsibility of the researcher not to harm the participants. Participants must be informed beforehand about the potential impact of the investigation. There must be an effort on the part of the researcher to avoid harm, an attempt to minimise if such harm is expected afterwards, but the participants must be informed on everything and be given the opportunity to discontinue or withdraw from participation if they wanted to do so.

1.11.8. Maintaining Non–judgmental and Non–discrimination.

The researcher must maintain non-judgmental attitude to the participant. The researcher must also not discriminate. All participants are handled the same.

1.12. LIMITATIONS OF THE STUDY.

In any research studies, limitations are expected. Limitations could involve the following.

• Language Barrier

According to Boxill et. al (1997:67) it is advised that researcher and the participant must share a common language in order for the data collected to be genuine. In such cases, an interpreter can be requested.

However, interpretation is likely to be faulty and cannot be reliable enough to provide an authentic interpretation of data.

• Financial Constraints

A study can be funded with limited financial muscle. The researcher can be confronted with problems in travelling, and not being to reach out to all places included in the proposal research. Financial constraints can Jeopardise research process and study may take longer than arranged, because the researcher has to go back to the drawing board to minimise financial needs.

• Respondents expectations

Respondents are likely to expect unwanted demands, such as,

20

for example, respondents might be of the idea that you have to alleviate their pain and suffering and hopes are raised that an immediate psychosocial intervention is required. Such limitations are likely to derail progress.

- Access Roads

In some cases researcher has to be conducted in remote rural areas where access roads are impassable. Travelling to such places becomes a limitation.

1.13. DEFINITION OF CONCEPTS/TERMS.

In research one needs to highlight concepts that will be utilised in the study so as to give more clarity to readers of the text on what to expect. Clarification of concepts is a continuing process in social research. In some forms of qualitative research, concept clarification is key element in data collection hence it is important to address conceptualization at the beginning of any study design. Concepts that will be utilised in the research study must involve literature concepts and methodological concepts to enable the reader to understand what will be included in the entire text of the research .Powers, Meenaghan and Toomey (1985) indicate that a conceptualization is the refinement and specification of abstract concepts and operationalization is the development of specific research procedure operations that will result in empirical observation representing those concept in the real world. According to E.Babbie & J.Mouton the process of concept has to be defined in the beginning of any research study for operationalisation.

1.14 CONCLUSION

The above chapter serves as initial guidelines to post-graduate student because it highlights the most crucial areas of what research entails. It has clarified how a student can be able to choose a topic relevantly and with precision whilst at the same time a student is in a position not to loose the trend or the sight of the research part that a student has selected. Researchers who will benefit are honours, master's and doctoral students.

The introductory part of this book throws more light on how the students are expected to present in relation to the problem of the research topic.

Problem statement poses a lot of interpretation of the various authors on the research topic both nationally and internationally. Various authors highlight varied objectives, purpose, strategies and findings of the study that have been utilised on the selected topic.

Apart from the problem statement there must be varied reasons to choose this specific study and also the objectives of the study.

The study might be significant in one way or the other in that particular demacarcation area of the study chosen. For example, a specific community might be engulfed in poverty and crime. The researcher may be interested to know why people who are poor indulge in criminality.

Ethical considerations are equally of importance in research as they render research process to be authentic and admissible to the participants or subjects during data gathering process.

Researcher must be aware of limitations likely to occur during the research process. Research students must realise that stating limitations in the study demonstrate an honest, reliable and authentic research study which gives a very good impression to the promoter that the student understand what entails to a research study.

Finally, concepts need to be described in context because conceptualizing demonstrates knowledge of the literature review undertaken by the student, including methodological concepts/terms that will be utilized in the study.

CHAPTER TWO

2.1. Literature review.

Literature review is fundamental in any research study because it provides relevant information in the research undertaken by other researchers. As a starting point, Welman, Sj Kruger (2005) indicates that a student has to familiarize himself /herself with the chosen topic by doing research review on the relevant literature of the study in the library. It is also important to review literature even before a research proposal is undertaken. The researcher obtains not only the text message but is also able to lean on the findings and recommendations of the study. Literature review enables the researcher to get an in-depth information of the topic to be researched. In the process the researcher identifies formulated research subjects with precision.

Before the researcher ventures to undertake the study, she/he lists heading or key areas that relate to the chosen research topic. Heading and key areas relating to the topic can help the student researcher retrieve information from the classified library catalogue which enables the student researcher to compile the correct information relating to the target research topic. By compiling a review of the research text with findings will give the student guidance to start planning the research study towards writing of the dissertation and theses successfully.

Collins (1990), provides the following objectives of the literature review:

- To bring to light investigators similar to your own research study thereby showing how other researchers tackle the situation in question.

- To suggest methods of managing problematic situations similar to your own study problem.

- To bring to light data resources that you may not have been aware of.

- To introduce you to major research authors.

- To put your own study in historical and associational perspective (i.e. its relevance to the current state of knowledge) by looking at the various ways in which your problem area was dealt with by others.

- To provide you with new ideas and approaches that may not have occurred to you.

- To assist you in evaluating your own research efforts by comparing them with the efforts of others.

- To help establish the limits of the investigation (ie to demarcate the problem area).

- To help you prepare methodology of your study.

In concluding the student is required to have a conclusion which might address either be a summary of the chapter or an evaluative comments about the literature review. That will demonstrate that the student has grasped the literature very well.

CHAPTER THREE

3.1. RESEARCH METHODOLOGY.

3.1.1. Research design.

Research design is the method utilised to obtain information. According to Mouton and Marais (1985:38) research design is the overall plan or strategy by which questions are answered and are hypothetically tested according to Reid & Smith (1981:64). According to McKendrick (1990:256) a universal characteristic of research plans is flexible. However with the purpose of the research design being a plan to provide answers to social questions, unexpected conditions in the social situation could rise to fresh questions. Therefore the research plan is subject to alterations. There are various types of research designs, they are the following.

3.1.2. Explanatory design

3.1.3. Single-subject design

3.1.4. Evaluative design

3.1.5. Experimental design

3.1.6. Descriptive design

3.1.7. Observational design

3.1.8. Exploratory design

3.1.9. Unit of analysis

3.1.2. Explanatory design

According to Rubin & Babbie (1989) explanatory design is to explain things as they happen. For example, to report as to why some cities have higher crime rates than others is a case in explanation.

In explanatory design, a researcher has explanatory purpose if a researcher wishes to know why an antinuclear demonstration ended in a violent confrontation with police, as opposed to simply describe what happen in case of a descriptive design. Another example of an explanatory design might be 'why people want to vote for the ANC and not for the DA.'

3.1.3. Single subject design.

Single subject design can be implemented by social work practitioner as part of a clinical practice. Direct service practitioners can be expected to become scientific practitioners. A practitioner routinely monitors client progress by the social behaviour takes place shortly when the child is about to be placed in one or the other parent and it is done repeatedly, the practitioner is helped in better understanding the causes of the target problem and be able to develop appropriate strategy or intervention.(Rubin & Babbie1989).

According to Fouche & Schurink (2011:322) case-study in research design enables the researcher to explore the effectiveness of the programme based on the experience of the case-studies.

3.1.4. Evaluative design.

Evaluative design seeks to assess the effectiveness of a programme in an established project. There are various types of evaluative designs. Rubin& Babbie (1990:400) highlight the outcome effectiveness as one of the evaluative approaches, which is called (goal-attainment model). Outcome and Effectiveness evaluation approach.

seeks to determine its effectiveness and whether or not mission and the goal is achieved. e.g. Evaluating a community project namely 'Masincedane ' in the Ntabankulu District of the Eastern Cape.'

3.1.5. Experimental design.

<u>**FIGURE 0NE (1)**</u>

DIAGRAM OF BASIC EXPERIMENTAL DESIGN.

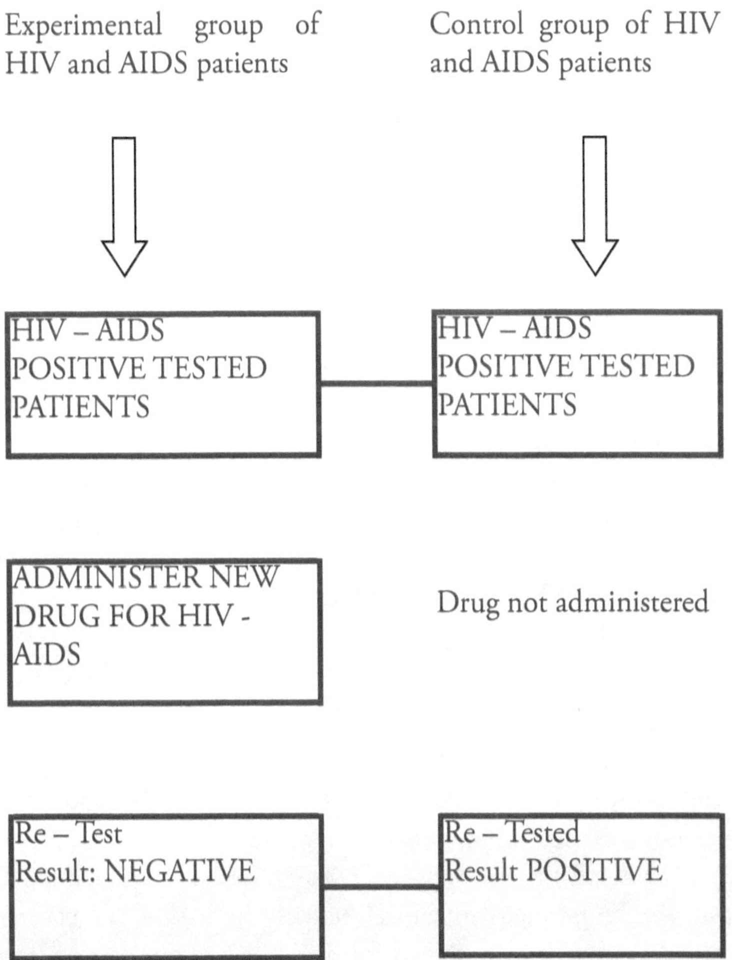

In the above figure HIV–AIDS patients (Experimental group) and HIV–Aids (control group) both are tested and found positive. In the experimental group, a new drug to cure HIV–AIDS was administered to the experimental group and not administered to the control group.

3.1.6 Descriptive design.

Descriptive design is intended to describe an event or situation. Scientific descriptions are more accurate and precise than casual description. Rubin & Babbie (1990:87).

3.1.7. Observational design.

In observational design there are two types of observation namely, simple observation and participant observation. In simple observation a researcher observes as an outsider, whereas in participant observation the researcher forms part and parcel of the group to be studied.(Babbie & Mouton :2005:292).

3.1.8. Exploratory design.

Exploratory research design is defined as research conducted to study a topic that is relatively unknown. According to Newman(1997):20) the purpose of research design is to enable researchers to familiarize themselves with the basic facts relating to the topic of the study, to formulate a clear understanding of it, and to determine the necessity of undertaking further research on the topic.

3.1.9. Unit of analysis.

According to De Vos(1998) unit of analysis is identified as individuals, collectives, organizations (formal and informal). A close look at the unit of analysis lead to a researcher's decision to modify the unit in order to suit the researcher's goal better. It is therefore important to realise that the choice of a unit of analysis is inevitable, and that it must be consciously built into the process of formal problem formulation.

On the other end, Babbie & Mouton (2005:84) are of the opinion that the unit of analysis refers to the 'WHAT' of your study i.e. What object, phenomenon, entity, process or event the researcher is interested investigating. Babbie & Mouton et.al. give an example of conducting an empirical research problems such as studying human behaviour. Both authors DeVos (1998) and Rubin& Babbie (2005) provide similar views about the unit of analysis using different versions with similar interpretation of a unit of analysis.

Unit of analysis may refer to an individual, a family, group's organizations and institution. According to Babbie, E.& Mouton, J. (2005:85-86) Individuals human beings are perhaps the most typical units of analysis to be studied for social scientific research. However there is no limit of what or who can be studied. Social groups can also be a unit of analysis for scientific research. A researcher can study a group as a unit of analysis. A group consists of individuals within the group and can be studied. Similar situation with the family members who are individuals, and organizations and Institutions who consists of employees who are individuals can be the subjects of study. Other units of analysis are characteristics of individual in a group, a family, an organization and institution can be studied scientifically. At times social action can be a unit of analysis in a situation where a researcher is less interested to study individuals. In other words unit of analysis can involve an object, a phenomena, entity, a process, social artefact, or an intervention.

The above description of the unit of analysis will be useful to the research student as it gives the student more clarity on selection of respondents.

3.2 SAMPLING.

Sampling is done by a researcher when he/ or she would like to select respondents from a given population. Sample size is guided by the population size and also by the nature of the research study. According to Arkava & Lane (1983:27) sample size is the element of the population considered for factual inclusion in the study or it can be viewed as sub-set of measurements drawn from a population which is key to research. A sample is intended to understand the population by an inference. Seaberg(1998:240) describes a sample as a small portion of the total set of objects or event or persons which together comprise the subject of the study.

The above authors description of sampling summarily explain sampling as process of selecting a specific number of respondents from a designated population in a community.

There are two types population of sampling, namely, probability and non-probability sampling.

3.2.1. Probability sampling

The basic principle of probability sampling is its representative-ness of a population, only if each number of a population has the same probability of appearance in the sample. There are two advantages of probability sampling; it is easy to estimate the amount of errors involved when using statistics and also it is easy to get an estimate values that are obtainable from the entire population. (Rubin & Babbie, 1997.)

Probability sampling is based on randomization. In general terms probability sampling involves selection of persons from a population in the form of random procedure. The following are the various types of probability sampling

- **Simple random sampling**

Kerlinger (1986:110) states that random sampling is a method of drawing a sample in such a way that each member in the population has an equal chance of selection. For example, a researcher might require a sample size of 20 respondents from High school. In a given population of 40 pupils from each class of four, the researcher will select five(5) in each class of four so that there is an equal chance of selecting respondents from the intended study.

- **Systematic Sampling**

Hoinville, Jowell & Associates (1978:61) cites selection as a selection that is done accordingly to a particular interval as determined by the researcher e.g. on a given population the researcher might decide to select one case after every fifth or tenth case until the required sampling is reached.

- **Stratified Random Sampling**

According to Van der Walt(1984:61) stratification is suitable in a universe where strata is exclusive and whose members are homogeneous in terms of their characteristics such as home language, race or age. The desired number of persons is selected within each of the different stratas. Selection will be random in each strata. According to Mitchell & Jolley, 2001:497 this kind of sampling is mainly used to ensure that different groups or segment of a population acquire sufficient representation in the desired sample. The desired number of persons is selected proportionally in each of the different strata.

- **Cluster sampling**

Rubie & Babbie (1998) is of the opinion that selection is based on national sample. For example, a researcher might select from a national sample of churches e.g. selection of domination, geograghical region, or urban or rural location. According to Sarantakos, (2000), cluster sampling has the advantage of concentrating in one geographical area and thus is cost-effective and also saves time.

- **Panel Sampling.**

A fixed panel of people is selected for a particular project. These people are supposed to be the representation of a particular relevant population (Rubin & Babbie, 1998). For example, if the researcher wants to see or know if the community is satisfied with health services the researcher will interview headman and chiefs only on the panel in order to gain the required information.

3.2.2. Non-probability sampling

In non-probability sampling method the researcher cannot estimate the probabilities associated with selection of different sample size. The consequences of using non-probability sampling is most likely to be biased in unknown ways because the researcher cannot estimate the error involved in the use of sample statistics as estimates of population parameters. Inferences made from non-probability sampling are very risky.

- **Accidental sampling**

Bailey(1994-94) Collins(1990:207) Gabor,(1993:162) indicate that this type of sampling is convenient because respondents are usually those who are nearest and most easily accessible e.g. a man in the street can be interviewed at first sight.

- **Purposive/judgmental sampling**

The researcher has a purpose to research specific study. This type of sampling is entirely based on the judgment of the researcher. For example, the researcher may take the views of educated youth in a focussed box in the clinic and present them as he/she believes that views from educated youth are more representative of the sample the researcher wants.

- **Quota sampling**

A sampling of a particular category is utilised. A cross section of the population is involved in selecting the particular category of persons accordingly to the distribution of the categories. (Babbie 1990:98).

- **Snowball sampling**

In snowballing the researcher approaches a single case who is involved in the phenomena for investigating. The person investigated may be requested to identify other people. The researcher continues with process until a sufficient number of respondents are complete (Baker, 1988:159).

- **Target sampling**

In target sampling the emphases is on hidden problems in hidden population. Sampling can be done by observation or perusing documents in which the number of respondents can be determined. The researcher needs to exercise a flexible approach in this particular sampling. (Water & Biernacki, 1989:427)

- **Dimensional sampling.**

Dimensional sampling is viewed by Bailey,(1994:95), as a multi-dimentional form of quota sampling that are of interest to the investigation. In this method only a few cases are studied in depth. With this method it is unlikely to miss out certain variables. For example, a researcher is able to specify each and every variable in the population relating to health issues in the community.

3.2.3. Sample size.

According to Montello & Paul(2006:155) it is important for researchers to address the most important aspect of the sample size before the commencement of the data collecting process. Basically sampling is selected from a given population. whose size can be determined appropriately for probability purposes. The bigger the population the bigger the sampling size

3.2.4. Data gathering

Data collection is a method that can help a researcher to gather information about that specific area of study. There are various methods of data gathering used. According to De Vos (2005:175) when collecting data open questions give the respondent the opportunity of writing any answer in the open space. A researcher used open–ended questions in order to learn and determine how a respondent thinks open questions enabled the researcher to explore the variable better and obtain some idea of the spectrum possible responses whereas De Vos (et al)indicate that closed questions offer the respondent the opportunity of selecting one or more response choices from a number provided. Follow up questions are posed to allow more information to the previous questions.

It is therefore conclusive that both open and closed questions in collecting data have positive outcome. The following are the various methods of data collection relevant to qualitative approach.

3.2.5. Participant observation.

- Participative Action research

- Self Administered questionnaires

- Face to face interview surveys

- Telephone interviews

- Available record &

- Mailing

- Audio-visual method.

3.3.5.1. Participate observation.

Participant observation has two ways of observing. The first is covert

observation. It involves research that is done without aware-ness of the group under research study though the process is likely to contra-indicate ethical issues. Covert observation has its disadvantages and advantages. The researcher is likely not to be protected especially if the researcher is observing a de-viant group which may, at times resort to violence. While on the other end covert observation has its advantages as it makes research easy to conduct on a group that is being observed though there is need to ensure that the researcher has to have a debriefing of the participants after the covert observation.

Overt observation refers to a situation where the researcher is open about his/her intention to conduct research. All the members of the group are made aware of the research study process. Overt observation has its disadvantages and advantag-es. The disadvantage of overt observation might be associated with participants who might change their normal behaviour because the participants are aware that they are being studied thus distorting the outcome of the research findings. While on the question of an advantage, the researcher is likely to be honest with the participants overcoming ethical issues of deception or lack of informed consent. Thus the observation is kept at an objective state and free from bias.

Participant Observation is much utilised by most researchers. According to De Vos (1998:308) participant observation enables the researcher to observe with eye contact and facial expression. Therefore researcher is part and parcel of the respondents. Jorgensen (1989:22) indicates that field notes are to be utilised for recording because it is unwise to rely on memory. Field notes are helpful to the researcher because they give a detailed account of what occurred. Researchers get the opportunity to collect data in a natural setting.

3.2.6. Participant action research.

In participatory research people involved in the situation that is being studied are enabled in partnership with researchers and other role – players to become actively involved in collective efforts to address and solve their social problems. (C.F. Rahman, 1993:50)

3.2.7. Self-administered questionnaire

The researcher provides an instrument tool which is a questionnaire to the respondents who are expected to respond to questions independently. The questionnaire is given to respondents who can read and write.

3.2.8. Face-to-face Interview.

Face to face interviews are the most common methods of collecting survey data. The researchers ask questions orally from respondents and answers are recorded.

The interviews are explicit in obtaining information from another during a structured conversation based on a pre – arranged set of questions.

(Babbie & Mouton 2005:249). According to Rubin & Babbie (1989:322)

interview surveys, as a method of collecting data is more pliable rather than asking respondents to read questionnaires. The interview survey is also advantageous in attaining higher responses faster than mail surveys.

3.2.9. Telephone Interviews

Telephone interviews, though used are limited to people who have interviews. By definition this type of interview is limited to a certain social class excluding the poor. However, telephone interview may be advantageous because it is cheaper and less costly rather than driving several km to interview a respondent and only to find nobody in the house (Rubin & Babbie, 1989)

3.2.10. Available Records

According to the States Record Act,1997, a record is a piece of written, printed, graphic, or pictorial matter, a disk, tape recorded or electronic process evidence about the past that provides information which serves an official record, more especially an account of an act or occurrence kept in writing. Records can be stored in different forms, from paper-based document and reports to e-mails, faxes, cd's, maps, web pages, photographs and films.

When a student is actually doing practice in an agency, as a research student, there is the possibility of collecting data from the recorded case studies. For example, if a student research student is doing research on the frequency of teenage pregnancy among the youth of Mdantsane, it becomes easy for a student researcher who has been handling cases of pregnant teenagers in the agency to collect data from the available records of the agency.

Records are important because they are used in the following ways:

- To provide evidence of actions and decisions

- To support accountability and transparency

- To comply with legal and regulatory obligation, including employment, contract and financial law as well as Protection Act and freedom of information Act.

- To support decision-making process.

- To protect the interests of staff, students and other stakeholders.

- To have an evidence of communication

- To provide evidence of work activities by making them available to the public.

There are many types of available records. They are the following:

- **Journal Articles**

Journal Articles are the results of academic papers published in scientific journals. Journal articles are peer-reviewed by experts in the same research field to ensure that the content is suitable for publication in scientific journals.

- **Conference papers**

Conference papers are original contributions to scientific literature published in scientific conference proceedings.

- **Reviews**.

The reviews are a category of scientific documents that provide summary of research on a topic extracted from documents of specific journals.

- **State records.**

State records are kept in or received and stored by person in the course of the exercise of official functions in a public office, or for the use of a public office.

- **Official Records**

An official record is either a University's or any Institution's records of its business activities. Official records must be captured on official file in the formal records management system where official records are recorded on the data base.

- **Unofficial records**

These are daily records kept within an office that can be duplicates or drafts of record already held in an official data base of the Institution.

(Savage T.I. 1996)

3.2.11. Mailing.

According to Grinnel & Williams (1990:216 – 217) mailed questionnaires can be sent to respondents with the hope that the questionnaires will be returned. The advantages of mailed questionnaires are that the costs are relatively low. The respondents also enjoys the freedom of completing the questionnaire and the information can be obtained from a large number of respondents within a brief period of time (Syman,1984:83) on the other hand mailed questionnaires can be disadvantageous and have limitations with other respondents failing to return the questionnaires. At times some of the respondents might find difficulty in understanding questions asked in the questionnaires.

3.2.12. Audio-Visual Method.

According to Greef, M. (2005), data collection in audio-recording during interviews requires transcribing themes and sub-themes. It is also essential to analyse data before data is summarized, interpreted and compared with the literature study.

Video–tape recording is a method of data gathering. There are three (3) most common audio–visual methods namely:

- Films

- Photographs

- Visual method

- Filming as a visual research method

Film has a unique ability to capture visible phenomena objectively. It requires the documentation of the time, place and subject of the filming which is focused on researcher's intent and interest. (Marchall & Rossman, 1989:86 – 87).

The advantage of filming in collecting data is the ability to record events in their natural setting. On the practical side filming can have disadvantages such as being expensive requiring technical experts. (Marshall & Roman 1989).

- Photography as a research method

According to Harper (1994) there are two types of photography research method, namely the documentary photography and the real life situation of patients. In documentary photography all images must be recognised. In document art photography, the researcher must remember when taking pictures that the information gathered is organised and is able to gather information that can be verbalised. In reality life situation photographs can be utilised to portray children's experiences.

3.3. VALIDITY & RELIABILITY

3.3.1. Validity

The term validity refers to the extent to which an empirical measure adequately reflects the real meaning of the concept under consideration (Babbie & Mouton 2005:122). According to Kanyemba (1212; 61) validity simply refers to the accuracy of a measure. Validity can be explained the following under the following characteristics namely:-

- Criterion - related/predictive validity and

- Content validity

Criterion – related validity sometimes called prediction validity and is based on some external criterion. For example the validity of the matric results is shown in its ability to predict the academic success of the University students. (Babbie & Mouton, 2005:123)

Content validity refers to how much a measure covers the range of meanings included within the concept. For example, a test of mathematical ability cannot be limited to addition alone, but would also require inclusion of subtraction, multiplication division and so forth. (Babbie & Mouton et.al 2005).

3.3.2. Reliability

According to Nkanyemba (2012:61) reliability is concerned with the accurateness of the actual measuring instrument or procedure, for example, the researchers questionnaire can be compiled in such a way as to closely link with the content of the problem in the study, and make certain that the questions address what the researcher want to find out at the end of the study.

There are two types of reliability namely,

- Test–retest method

- Split-half method

3.3.2.1. Test–retest Method

In test method, it is appropriate to apply the same measurement more than once to determine reliability of the measure. For example subjects can be called upon to complete a questionnaire and subjects respond accordingly. Three months thereafter, a follow – up may be done by applying same questionnaire to same subjects. If the questionnaire was reliable on retest it is expected to give similar responses.

3.3.2.2. Split half Method

In split-half method, a researcher can draw up a questionnaire that contains two sets of subjects. What measure prejudice against women if the two sets of items measure people differently, that indicates that measurement has not been reliable because there is inconsistency in providing outcome of measurement.(Babbie & Mouton 2005:122)

3.4. CONCLUSION.

Research methodology has various phases of research, namely, research design, unit of analysis, sampling, data gathering and validity and reliability. Research design is intended to highlight various methods of obtaining information. Research design is therefore intended to provide answers to questions. The various types of designs illustrate varied approaches to get information in respect of the study.

Unit analysis is meant to identify subjects such as groups, families, organizations, or agencies that are the focus of the study.

Sampling is done by a researcher to select participants from a given population. Sampling is divided into two (2) categories, namely, non-probability and probability sampling. The two (2) divisions of sampling are utilized by the researcher depending upon what the research purport to study. Sample size is determined by the researcher on the bases of an inference to the entire target population. The outcome of the research will represent the ideals of the entire population which has been targeted by the researcher.

Validity and reliability also plays a major role in the outcome of the research process. Both validity and reliability tests authenticity and accuracy of the measure utilized by the researcher. For example, a questionnaire is likely to be erroneous depending upon the questions compiled and asked by the researcher from the respondents. Some of the questions asked may not conform to what is required in the process of examining the study problem. Erroneous outcome of the research is likely to affect the scientific requirement of the study problem which may give rise to a distorted probability outcome. However, it is important for students to identify validity and reliability of any study and be honest in disclosing such an error in compiling the dissertation/theses. For any student to disclose an error in his/her dissertation/theses demonstrates that the student is scientifically aware of the research outcome and the promoter will be in a position to respect and rely upon student's understanding of the empirical research process.

CHAPTER FOUR.

4.1. DATA ANALYSIS

TerreBlanche, Durrheim and Kelly (2006) have developed five (5) steps of analysing data. In the first (1st) step the author familiarise herself with the data by making notes and brain-storming. The second (2nd) step is to induce the themes based on the principle that underpin the material. Step three (3) involves coding the information gathered by grouping certain kinds of information in order to compare responses from participants. Step four (4) is to identify sub-issues and themes that emerge from coding and comparing the information. Step five (5) entails the final stage in which interpretation is made to make some meaning to the data at hand. With the five (5) steps one is able to understand the reliability and trustworthiness of the data analyses in providing authentic findings of the study.

Once data is gathered, the researcher has to analyse the data collected.

According to Creswell (194), data analysis is a process of inspection, cleaning, transforming and modelling data with the goal of highlighting useful information suggesting conclusions made after data gathering. Data analysis has multiple facets and approaches which encompass diverse techniques under a variety modalities.

There are two methods of analysis, namely:

4.1.1. Quantitative measure

4.1.2. Qualitative measure.

Quantitative data is process of presenting, and interpreting numerical data. Outcome of the interpretation of data often contains descriptive statistics and inferential statistics.

According to Bless & Higson Smith (2007) data analysis is the process of unlocking the information hidden in raw data and transforming it into something useful and meaningful. Descriptive statistics include measures of central tendency such as averages-mean, median and mode and measures of variability about the average(range and standard deviation) The latter give the reader a picture of the data collected and used in the research project. Inferential statistics are the outcomes of statistical tests, helping deductions to be made from the data collected to test hypothesis set relating findings to the sample of the entire population.

Montello & Sutton (2006:157) indicate that data analysis helps the researchers to achieve the four (4) scientific goals namely, description, explanation, exploratory & control.

The terms quantitative and qualitative measures are utilised in data analysis. Both quantitative and qualitative methods are empirical because both utilise experience and observation as a route to knowledge. They only differ in that quantitative methods are more concerned with maximising the objectivity and testing the validity of what we think we are observing, whereas qualitative methods are more concerned with subjectively tapping the deeper meanings of human experience (Rubin & Babbie 1989).

Fossey, Harvey, McDermott and Davidson (2002:723) state that in qualitative studies, qualitative research questions are used instead of hypotheses to "identify the initial focus of the inquiry". According to Newman (1977:20) qualitative data is a method in which data is a method in which data are expressed in the form of words. Donalek and Soldwisch (2004:356) are of the opinion that the qualitative researcher seeks to gain an in-depth understanding of the phenomena under study from the participant's point of view, because the participants are experts in their experiential world and are able to articulate and describe experiences and feelings until the researcher has gained a fuller understanding of the phenomena or part of the phenomena. Whereas Creswell (1994) cites qualitative research as being concerned with meaning, indicating how people can make use of their live experiences.

In qualitative data the approach is open–ended by probing questions in the process of interview. For example, the researcher asks a direct question which is followed by a response from a respondent.

The qualitative research allows researchers to identify issues from a perspective of a studies' participants and to understand the meaning and the interpretations that the latter attribute behaviour, events or objects, (Hennink, Hurter, and Bailey,2011:9).Qualitative research is by nature and function mainly exploratory and descriptive,(Marshall & Rossman in Ritchie& Lewis, 2005:27-28). It is also understood that qualitative research affords the researcher the opportunity to unpack issues and to explore and describe how they are understood by those connected with them. It was with this in mind that the researchers employed an explorative, descriptive and contextual design.

Quantitative method can be presented in various forms such as tables, graphs, figures, and pie chart. (Kanyemba 2012)

Below are examples of a quantitative data and a qualitative data is presented. First is the quantitative data which demonstrates a table.

An example of a table is the following:

TABLE ONE.

Presentation of Gender

Variables	Percentages	Frequency
Male	50%	25%
Female	50%	25%
Total	100%	50%

GRAPH ON FAMILY BASED APPROACH

Preference to reduce Poverty

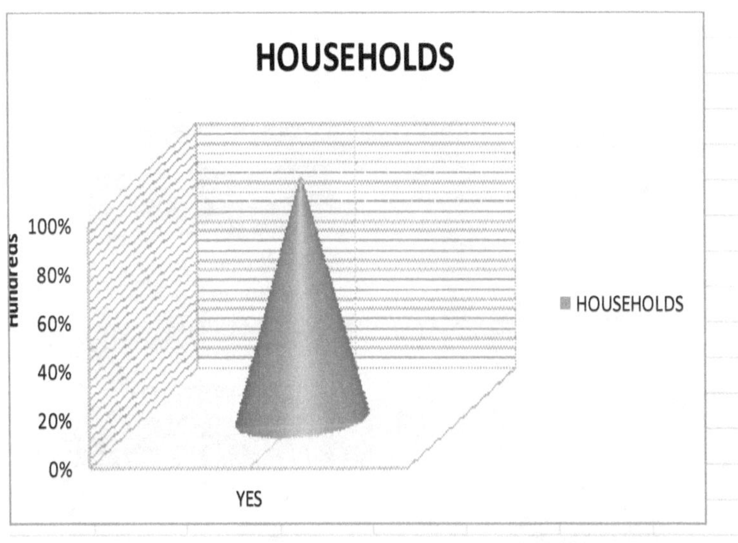

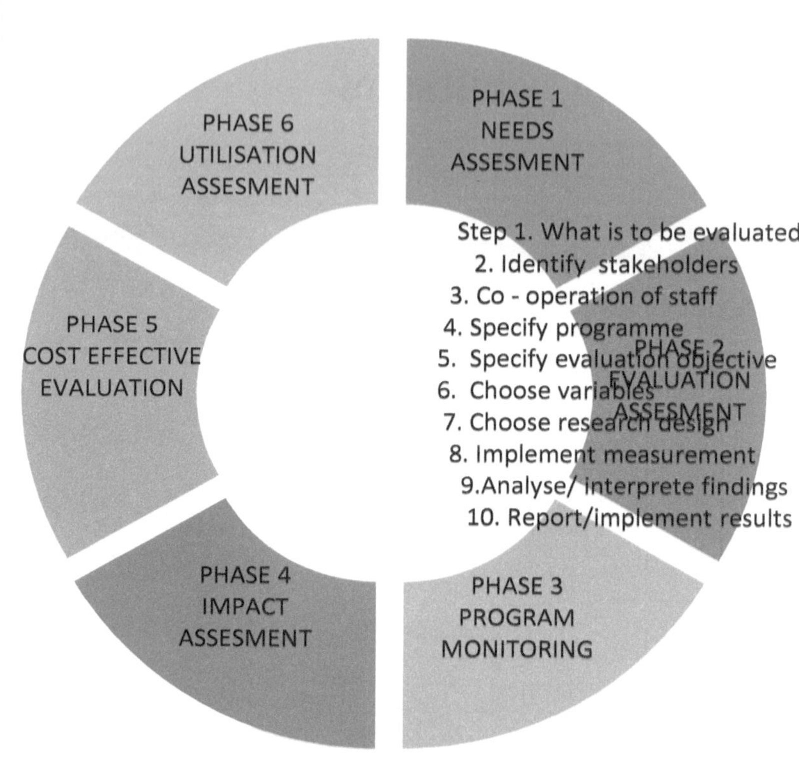

[SOURCE: McKendrick, 1989]
The Integrated Model of Program Education (IMPE)

PIE CHART

Below is a pie Chart on illiteracy level of Education:

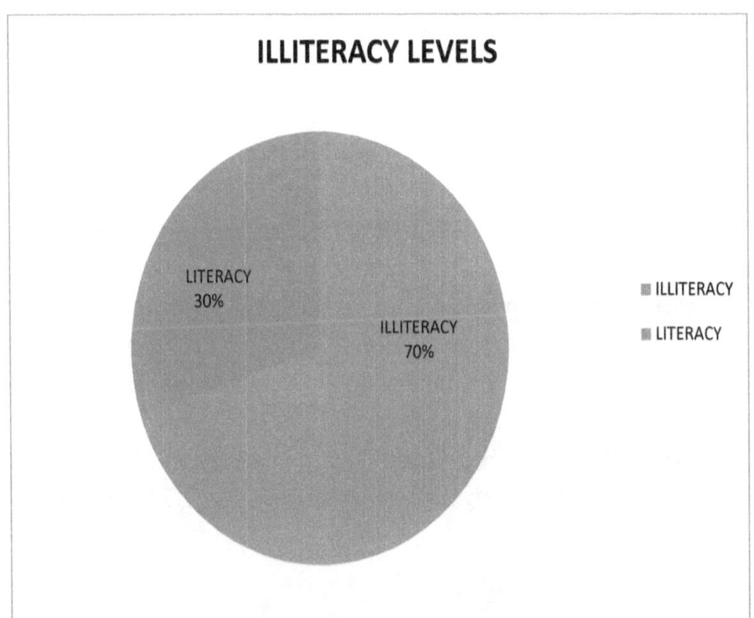

Above illiteracy levels are found to be low in rural areas presenting 70% illiteracy compared to urban areas, which records 30% literate people. It is therefore clear that qualitative data and quantitative methods differ in the above presented formulation.

The above tables graphs, figures and pie chart demonstrate examples for a quantitative data presentation.

Paton (2002), is of the opinion that qualitative approach enables the researchers to obtain a rich and in-depth understanding of the phenomena being studied. Qualitative data is a method of collecting data by posing direct questions from the respondents. Qualitative data relies on some form of interview as its primary method of collecting data. According to Miles & Huberman (1994:6), qualitative data is distinctive by a researcher's attempt to capture data on the perception of local actors from the inside through the process of deep attention of empathic understanding and of suspending or bracketing pre-conceptions about the topics under discussion.

Newman (2003:171) is of the opinion that qualitative research approach collect data in the form of words, sounds, visual images or objects. Whereas Mugenda & Mugenda (1992:20) refers to qualitative approach as a source of well-grounded rich description and explanation of processes in identifiable context. Mugenda et.al further indicates that qualitative data also encompasses the use of data collection technique that include observation, interviews and documentary reviews. The researcher is therefore able to extract in-depth information which cannot be solicited with the use of quantitative data technique.

Below are examples of a qualitative data presentation when a researcher collects data from a respondent.

Respondent one (1)

 Question from the researcher:

Do you think 'SHARE organization is a sustainable organization?

Answer from a respondent:

Yes; I see SHARE as a sustainable organization because it has been in existence for twelve (12) years and it is being supported by the government.

Respondent two (2)

Question from the researcher:

Are you convinced that service providers of the various programmes are qualified for the various programmes of the organization 'SHARE'?

Answer from the respondent:

Yes; service providers are qualified for the various programmes because their delivery of service is satisfactory.

The above two examples clarify the difference between a quantitative data and a qualitative data and students will be able to apply the two measures of data's appropriately and with precision.

4.2. CONCLUSION.

Data analysis has various steps to take in data processing. There are two (2) methods that are utilized in data analysis, namely, qualitative and quantitative methods. When analysing data, a researcher has to prepare questions to be asked from the respondents which require wording response. Qualitative data is mostly used at a senior level of post-graduate studies. Qualitative method is able to obtain in-depth information which will be crucial to the outcome of the study. Quantitative method presents tables, charts, graphs and figures which are more illustrative than the usage of words.

58

CHAPTER FIVE.

5.1 FINDINGS AND RECOMMENDATIONS.

The findings and recommendations of the study demonstrate that the objectives of the study have been achieved partly or wholly.

Hence, in view of the findings of the study it is essential to revisit the aim and the objectives to determine how far the objectives have been accomplished.

Recommendations are therefore proposed based on the finding of the study.

5.2. TIME FRAME.

Student is expected to present time frame for the completion of the Dissertation/Thesis. The time frame will be determined by the rules and the regulations of the various universities/Colleges.

5.3. RESEARCH FUNDING.

The student is expected to apply for research funding once the proposal is accepted. A student can get funding from a variety of sources other than the University where the student is registered.

At the end of the text references must be included to demonstrate the number of books, journals or any relevant documents the researcher might have perused.

Annexures must also follow the bibliography, the following are some of the annexures that can be included:

A contract letter from an organization, agency, an institution or any place where research was done.

A map representing demarcation area of the study, or any related and relevant document to the research study.

Finally findings and recommendations provide outcome of the entire research study. It enables the researcher to achieve the intended goals of the study. The researcher is able to reflect on the set objectives of the study and assess and determine whether the intended aim and the objectives have been achieved accordingly. Hence a student is required to re-visit the aims and the objectives in the last chapter of the text when presenting the findings. Findings of the study also meets the hypothetical outcome of the study and the extent of the hypotheses.

Recommendations are presented by the researcher on the bases of identified gaps of the study. On the bases of these gaps what needs to be done? The researcher has to recommend interceptive strategies in order to remedy the researched problem of the study.

Time frame is equally an important factor in the study. Time frame instils student's commitment to complete the study timeously. Time schedule is also important as it also helps to adhere to research funding.

SUMMARY.

The book highlights key areas of the research so that students are able to understand how to organize their proposal in preparation for the dissertation/thesis.

In conclusion, researchers/students doing research at honours, masters and doctoral studies are to map their chapters as follows:

In chapter one(1) data is presented by highlighting the overall introduction and orientation in terms of the statement of the study, rational of the study, demarcation area of the study, hypothesis, justification of the study, and the aim and the objectives of the study.

In chapter two (2) focus is on the literature review with reference to the chosen topic.

In chapter three(3) study continues on the literature review but with a focus on intervention strategies posed by other authors/researchers on the specific topic.

N/B. Chapter three (3) is included at masters and doctoral levels of the study on the above-stated literature review.

In chapter four(4) data is presented on the research methodology in relation to the research design, sampling and data gathering.

In chapter five (5) data analysis is presented quantitatively and qualitatively.

In chapter six (6) findings and recommendations are presented based on the content previously addressed in this text. However, having six (6) chapters is not cast in stone. Additional chapters can be included depending upon the nature and volume of the dissertation/thesis. It is generally common especially at the doctoral level of study that more data can be collected which will require more chapters. 62

In conclusion, it is hoped that students at honours, masters and doctoral level of study will find this book helpful and more handy to read and follow processes of research without difficulty. Promoters will also find the book helpful for them as well in supervising their students.

BIBLIOGRAPHY

1. Research publishers, Allyn Bacon. Inst. Massachussets. Publishers, Allyn & Bacon Inc: Massachusetts.

2. BABBIE, E.R. (2013,). **The Basics of Social Research,** Brooks & Cole Publishers.

3. BABBIE, E.R. (2012). **The Practice of Social Research**, Brooks & Cole Publishers.

4. BABBIE, E. & MOUTON, J. (2005). **The Practice of Social Research**,

5. BABBIE & MOUTON, J., (2010). **The Practise of Research,** Oxford University

6. BAILEY, E.P. & POWELL, P.A. (1987). **Writing Research Papers: A Practical Guide.** Rinchart & Wilson Publishers: New York.

7. BLESS, C. & HIGSON-SMITH, C. (1997). **Fundamentals of Social Research Methods: Social Research Perspective,** Juta & Co. Ltd   Publishers: Kenwyn.

8. BLESS, C. & HIGSON, C. & SITHOLE, L. (2013) 5th edition, **Fundamentals of Social research Methods,** Juta & Co. Publishers: Cape Town.

9. BOTTORFF, L.L. (1994). **Using videotaped recording in Qualitative research,** Morse, J.M.,(Ed). **Critical Issues in Qualitative research Methods.** Thousand Oaks Publishers: Saga.

10. I.C. & WINT, E. (1997). **Introduction to Social research Methods, Introduction to Social Research Methods,** Caneo University West: Indies.

11. COLLINS, K.J. & SPES, G.M. (1998). **Case- Study of an Adult Survivor of Sexual Molestation.** Social Work Journal 34(2) 191 – 205. SAGE publications:

13 .DE VOS, A.S., (Editor) 1998. **Research at Grass Roots: A primer for the Caring profession.** J.L. van Schaik Academic publishers. Pretoria.

14. DONALEK, J.G. &SOLDWISCH, S., (2004) **Demystifying Nursing Research.**

15. GOGO, N.J., (1988-1989). **Kwanobuhle Community Assessment Survey,** SHARE: Uitenhage.

16. GRAY, D.E., 2009, **doing Research in the real world.** Sage publishers: London.

17. GRAVELLE, F.J. & FORZANO, L.B., (2003). **Research Method for the Sciences behavioural sciences,** Thomson Wadsworth Publishers: London.

18. GREEF, M., (2005. **Information Collection Interviewing:** In De Vos A.S. (ed) **Research at Grass-roots for the Social science and Human service profession.** (4th eds) Van

Schaik publishers: Pretoria.

19. GRINNEL, R.M., (2001). **Social Work Research and Evaluation.**, F.E Peacock Publishers: Illinois.

20. GRINNEL, R.M., & WILLIAMS, M., (1990). **Research in Social Work: A Primer.** Peacock Publishers: Itasca.

21. HARPER, D., 1994). **On the authority of the image: Visual methods at the crossroads**. In Denzil, N.K. & Lincoln, Y.S. (Eds), Handbook **of Qualitative Research.** Thousand Oaks Publishers: Sage.

22. HENNINK, M., HURTER, I., & BAILEY, A., (2011). **Qualitative Research methods.** SAGE Publication: London.

23. HOINVILLE, G., & JOWELL, R., & ASSOCIATES, (1978). **Survey Research Practice,** Heinemann Education Publishers: London.

24. FOSSEY, E., HARVEY, C., MACDERMOTT, F. & DAVIDSON, L., (2002). **Understanding and evaluating qualitative research.** Published by Australian & New Zealand Journal of Psychiatry, 36:717-732.

25. FOUCHE, C.B., &SCHURINK, W., (2011). **Qualitative research designs: In Research at Grass-roots for Human service professions,** In De Vos A.S. (Ed) (4[th]ed), Van Schaik publishers: Pretoria.

26. KANYEMBA, P., (2012). **An investigation into the Challenges faced by children as Victims of HIV-AIDS with reference to the Nyandeni Area in the Eastern Cape: A Disser-**

tation submitted in fulfilment to the requirement for the **degree of Master of Social work**, published by Health Sciences Faculty: Mthatha.

27. KERLINGER, F.N., (1986) 3rd Ed. **Foundations of Behavioural Research,** Wordsworth: Hancourt.

28. LEEDY, P.D. (1997) 6th Ed. Practical Research: **A guide to the understanding of HIV-AIDS**, **Planning and designing,** Publisher, Upper Saddle River: Merill.

29.LEEDY,P.D.& ELLI, (2005) **Practical Research Planning and design,**9th edition, University of Northern Colorado (Emerita) University of New Hampshire publisher, Merill.

30. ROSMAN, G.B., (1989). **Designing qualitative Research,** publisher Newbury Park. CA: Sage.

31. ROYSE, D. (2011). **Research Methods in social work.** Brooks. Cole Centage: New York.

32. MARSHALL, C. &ROSSMAN, G.B.B. (1995). **Designing qualitative research,** SAGE publishers: Newbury Park.

33 .MBANDAZAYO, N.P. 2012). **Management of Community Projects. In Disadvantaged Communities in the Eastern Cape,** a thesis submitted for the degree of Doctor of Philosophy in Social work at the University of Stellenbosch.

34. MBANDAZAYO, N.P. (2012), **Community work and Development: A Research study on Developmental Approach to Communities.** Publishers, Vuga Books: Durban.

35 .MILES, M.B. & HUBERMAN, A.M. (1994), **Qualitative data analysis: An Expanded sourcebook,** thousand Oaks: SAGE.

36. McKENDRICK, B.W. (1989). **Introduction to social work in South Africa** Publishers, Owen Burgess: Pine Town.

37. MOUTON J., Marais, H.C. (1990), **'Basic Concepts in the Methodology of the Social Sciences.** Publisher, HSRC: Pretoria.

38. MONETTE, D.R.SULLIVAN, TJ. & DEJONG, C.R. (2011).**Applied Social research: A tool the Human Sciences,** / Cole Centage **learning:** New York.

39. NEWMAN, W.L. (1997). **Social Research Methods: Qualitative and quantitative Approach,** (edition) publisher, Ally & Bacon: Boston,

40. NTONJANE, N. (2013). **Family-based Approach-A strategy to alleviate Poverty in the eastern Cape, South Africa:** A dissertation submitted in fulfilment of the requirements for the degree of Master of social work (MSW), Health Sciences at WSU: Mthatha.

41. PATON, Q.R. (2002). **Qualitative research & Evaluation Methods,** SAGA Publications: California.

42. POWERS, G.T. MEENAGHAN, T.M. & TOOMEY (1985). **Practice-focussed research: Integrating human service practice and Research,** publisher, Prentice-Hall: New Jer-

sey.

43. RAHMAN, A., (1993). **People's self-determination: Perspective on Participatory Action Research**: London, Zed.

44. RICHER, J. & LEWIS, J. (2005) **Qualitative research practice: A guide to social service students & researchers**. SAGE publishers, Thousand Oaks:

45. ROYSE, D. (2004), **Research methods in social work, P**ublisher, Thomson Brooks /Cole: London.

46. REIDS, W.J. & SMITH, (1993). **Writing research reports**, Publisher, Itasca, IL. Peacock.

47. RICHTER, J. & LEWIS,J.(2005), **Qualitative research Practice: A** for **guide for social service students & researcher,** SAGE publication, thousand Oaks: California;

48. RUBIN, A. & BABBIE, E.R. (2010).8th Edition, **Research Methods for social** work. Publisher, Brooks & Cole: Hepsworth.

49. RUBIN, & BABBIE, (2010), **Essential Research methods for social work,** Publisher, Brooks/ Cole Centage Learning: New York.

50 .RUBIN, A. & BABBIE, E. (1989). **Research Methods for social workers**, Publishers, Belmont, CA: Wordsworth.

51. SAVAGE, T.I. (1996), **Observing Pharmacist at work: Qualifying the Hawthorn Effect**: Journal of Social and Administration.

52. SEABERG, J.R. (1988). **Utilizing sampling procedures: In Grinnel, R.M. Social work & Evaluation,** (3rd ed): Itasca, I.L. Peacock, 240-247.

53. SHABALALA, M.M. (2012). **An Investigation of the causes of Gender Based-Violence in KwaNongoma area.** A dissertation submitted in University of Zululand

54. TERRE'BLANCHE, M. DURRHEIM, K. & KELLY,(2006), **First Steps in Qualitative data analysis:** Terre Blanche, M & Painter. (eds). **Research in Practice, Applied methods for social sciences** (2nd eds) Cape Town: University of Cape Town Press. P.322-344.

55. THYLER, B. (2010), **The Handbook of social work research methods.** SAGE publication: Los Angeles.

56. WELMAN, J.C. & S.J. KRUGER, (2003) 2nd Ed. **Research Methodology** Publishers, Oxford University Press: South Africa.

57. WILLIAMS, D.A. / KARP, J.R. / DALPHIN & GRAY, S.G. (1982) 2nd Ed. **The Research Craft: An Introduction to Social Research Methods**, Publishers, Brown & Company, Boston/Toronto.

About the Author

PROFESSOR NOSINODI PATRICIA MBANDAZAYO.

Professor N.P. Mbandazayo is a retired professor. She retired in her position as the Head of the Department of Social work in WSU in South Africa in the Eastern Cape.

She is currently registered with the Association of Social workers in Private Practice which has enabled her to engage in Private Practice as a Social Worker.

She completed a Diploma in Community Work and Development in North Carolina University, Chapel Hill in the USA from 1980-1981.

She then registered a two-year Masters Degree in Social work at Adelphi University in New York USA from 1982 and completed the degree in 1984.

She registered PHD at the University of Stellenbosch completing the degree and graduating PHD in 2002.

She has gathered a lot of research work which enable her to be elevated to a position of professorship.

Research experience she has gathered has encouraged her in supervising MSW and PHD student in Social work in WSU in Social work and in the writing books.

Currently she is practicing as a private social work.

Also by N.P Mbandazayo

COMMUNITY WORK AND DEVELOPMENT. A Research Study on Development Approach to Community.

72